KT-225-010

OVERLOAD
STUDY GUIDE

How to Unplug, Unwind, and Unleash Yourself
from the Pressure of Stress

JOYCE MEYER

NEW YORK · BOSTON · NASHVILLE

Copyright © 2016 by Joyce Meyer

Cover design by Candace Gerard
Author photograph by David Dobson
Cover copyright © 2016 by Hachette Book Group, Inc.

All rights reserved. In accordance with the U.S. Copyright Act of 1976, the scanning, uploading, and electronic sharing of any part of this book without the permission of the publisher constitute unlawful piracy and theft of the author's intellectual property. If you would like to use material from the book (other than for review purposes), prior written permission must be obtained by contacting the publisher at permissions@hbgusa.com. Thank you for your support of the author's rights.

FaithWords
Hachette Book Group
1290 Avenue of the Americas
New York, NY 10104
faithwords.com
twitter.com/faithwords

First Edition: May 2016

FaithWords is a division of Hachette Book Group, Inc.
The FaithWords name and logo are trademarks of Hachette Book Group, Inc.

The publisher is not responsible for websites (or their content)
that are not owned by the publisher.

The Hachette Speakers Bureau provides a wide range of authors for speaking events. To find out more, go to www.hachettespeakersbureau.com or call (866) 376-6591.

Scriptures quotations marked (AMP) and (AMPC) are taken from *The Amplified Bible*, Old Testament, copyright © 1965, 1987 by The Zondervan Corporation. *The Amplified New Testament*, copyright © 1954, 1958, 1987 by The Lockman Foundation. Used by permission.

Scripture quotations marked (KJV) are taken from the King James Version of the Bible.

Scriptures noted (NIV) are taken from the *Holy Bible: New International Version* ®. Copyright © 1973, 1978, 1984 by International Bible Society. Used by permission of Zondervan Publishing House. All rights reserved.

Scripture quotations marked (NLT) are taken from the *Holy Bible*, New Living Translation, Copyright © 1996. Used by permission of Tyndale House Publishers, Inc., Wheaton, Illinois 60189. All rights reserved.

Scripture quotations marked (NKJV) are taken from the *New King James Version*. Copyright © 1979, 1980, 1982 by Thomas Nelson, Inc., Publishers.

ISBN: 978-1-4555-9654-6 (pbk.)

Printed in the United States of America

RRD-C

10 9 8 7 6 5 4 3 2 1

OVERLOAD
STUDY GUIDE

WITHDRAWN FROM STOCK

CONTENTS

I'm so excited about my book *Overload: How to Unplug, Unwind, and Unleash Yourself from the Pressure of Stress* and this companion study guide. I believe it can be an effective tool to help you learn how to manage and even eliminate some of the stress in your life because the principles it teaches are based on the Word of God. And God's Word—the Bible—is the source of wisdom and truth that will set you free and allow you to fulfill the plan God has for your life.

This workbook has been written to help you better understand and apply the principles discussed in *Overload*. I've dealt with stress in my life and I know you've experienced it in some ways, too. But we can take comfort in knowing that Jesus Christ understands the pressure of stress and He knows what we're going through. In the midst of all the pressures He endured while accomplishing His mission on earth, He remained peaceful and was never stressed out or overcome by the stress He experienced. That's why it's so important for us to seek the solution to manage and defeat stress by studying God's Word. It's the key to discovering how to have real peace and joy in your everyday life.

By using this workbook with the main book, you will go deeper in your understanding of what God's Word teaches us about managing our stress. I encourage you to pray and ask God to show you how to apply what you learn to your life. Make this a personal study that changes your approach to the challenges of everyday life.

Begin each chapter after you've read the corresponding chapter in *Overload*. Take time to prayerfully reflect upon and answer each question honestly and sincerely. Each section has been designed to help you contemplate the practical principles in the book so you can effectively put stress-reducing steps into action.

Get Started: Each chapter in the workbook begins with "Get Started." This section is designed to get you ready to focus on the theme of the chapter and the corresponding activities. It also provides time for you to review what you've committed to change as you go through the study and evaluate your progress.

Take the Load Off: This section gets to the heart of the chapter and offers suggestions to help you think more deeply about the book's content and biblical principles.

De-Stress Today: You are provided with action items centered around key themes in the chapter. This section is designed to give you practical ways to incorporate the principles from the chapter into your everyday life.

Remember…: Several key ideas from the chapter are listed to reinforce practical ways to de-stress. Consider memorizing these points or keeping them handy on a notecard to guide you throughout your day.

Prayer: Each chapter in the workbook closes with a prayer based on the practical action steps suggested. There is also room for you to write down your own prayer.

Just like any other changes you want to make, putting the lessons you learn in *Overload* to work in your life will take time and effort. But the results are well worth every bit of time and energy you invest to make it happen. As you look to God for the ability to do your part in the process and trust Him to do His part, you'll discover a more joy-filled, peace-filled life, unleashed from the pressure of stress!

OVERLOAD
STUDY GUIDE

Start Defeating Stress Today

Before you begin, please read the introduction and Chapter 1 in *Overload*.

Get Started

Read the quote that precedes Chapter 1: "Keep Calm and De-Stress." What are some methods you currently use to de-stress?

_____

_____

_____

Reread the list and write down the last time you recall doing one of these activities to de-stress. How effective was it?

_____

_____

_____

Think about the opening quote by Charles Spurgeon. Take a few moments to journal how anxiety has emptied you of today's strength and how you can regain your strength.

_____

_____

_____

Take the Load Off

Many people have contracted the stress virus . . . but they don't seem to realize it. Their friends and family see it. Their bosses and coworkers see it. Everyone around them knows that they're stressed out, but they're oblivious to it. They have not learned to recognize the symptoms of stress. They've gone about each day anxious, upset, worried, tense, and frustrated, and they've just accepted this as a part of life. It's their "new normal" (*Overload*, p. 3–4).

Take a "stress test" right now.

Review the last week. How many times have you felt:

_____ Anxious

_____ Upset

_____ Worried

_____ Tense

_____ Frustrated

What factors are causing your stress? Consider the stressors mentioned in Chapter 1. Put a check mark beside the stressors that apply to you or add your own.

_____ You're extremely busy.

_____ You're not resting properly.

_____ You're still dealing with emotional repercussions from negative incidents that occurred in childhood or as an adult.

_____ You're raising a child (or children).

_____ You're in the midst of the change of life or you have other health concerns.

Add more (e.g., troubled relationships, job issues, family concerns, financial distress, elder care, etc.).

When I saw my doctor, he told me I needed to make some changes to deal with the stress in my life. In *Overload*, I admit that I thought I was too strong for stress (p. 5). Do you feel this way? Why or why not?

Reread the effects of stress and the physical, emotional, and behavioral effects on pages 6–8.

Consider how the effects of stress impact your life and your well-being.

Now read John 10:10. Below, write down how the abundant life Jesus promises differs from a life filled with stress.

Let me encourage you: The stress you're facing doesn't mean there is something wrong with you. As a matter of fact, it just means you're human. As statistics show, men and women all around the world are feeling stress. But there is good news for us today—we don't have to live like the rest of the world. As believers, we have been promised a new life in Christ. We don't have to let stress rob us of our happiness. We can stand on the promises of God and trust that He is working out His great plan for our lives (p. 9).

De-Stress Today

God has a better life in store for you. A life full of laughter, contentment, provision, peace, and joy. But an important part of realizing all that God has for you is choosing to de-stress.

Check the steps you will take this week toward achieving the wonderful way of life God has planned for you. And then answer the questions that correspond with each step.

_____ 1. Seek Out Social Support
Who will you spend time with this week?

_____

_____ 2. Practice "Shrug Therapy"
List things you cannot control. How can you shrug them off?

_____

_____ 3. Find Your Comfort Zone...and Stay There
What is stealing your joy or your health? How can you find or return to your comfort zone?

_____

_____ 4. Nutrition, Proven Supplements, Healthy Diet, and Exercise
Evaluate your nutrition and fitness levels. What can you do to care for yourself better?

_____

_____ 5. Schedule Time to Relax
What do you like to do to unwind? What will you do this week to relax?

_____

Remember...

- We don't have to live as victims of stress. As believers, we have been promised a new, powerful, overcoming life in Christ.

Therefore, if anyone is in Christ, the new creation has come: The old has gone, the new is here! (2 Corinthians 5:17, NIV)

Prayer

Lord, I recognize that I have allowed stress to get to me. I have not always handled pressure well. I sometimes worry too much. I do not want to continue to live like this. I want to change. I want to experience the fresh, abundant new life You promise. Help me to make changes that will alleviate stress. Help me learn to relax and enjoy the life You've given me. Amen.

Make this prayer more personal in your heart by adding words of your own:

_____

_____

_____

Who's in Charge?

Before you begin, please read Chapter 2 in *Overload*.

Get Started

How did you do with the five Get Started steps from Chapter 1? What did you do to de-stress, and how did those activities impact you?

_____

_____

_____

Think about who you choose to trust. Be honest and write down your thoughts about where you place your trust.

_____

_____

_____

Read the opening quote by Corrie ten Boom (p. 19). Reflect on a train ride and how you sit still and trust the engineer when you go through a tunnel. How does this compare to how we should trust God, especially when things are dark or we are venturing down an unknown path?

_____

_____

_____

Take the Load Off

Read the list of "It's up to me" statements (p. 19). Check the ones that you've heard yourself say or think. Add any additional things you've said like this.

_____ It's up to me to make sure my children turn out great.

_____ It's up to me to keep the house clean and tidy all the time.

_____ It's up to me to figure out my future.

_____ It's up to me to pay for my past mistakes.

_____ It's up to me to provide all the things my children want.

_____ It's up to me to change my spouse.

_____ It's up to me to correct my coworkers.

_____ It's up to me to _____

_____.

When we think we need to do everything—or it won't get done, or it won't get done *right*—we do not leave room for God. The moment we begin to think, "I'm in control," rather than trusting that God is in control is the moment stress has an opening in our lives. God is good, and it is His desire that we place our trust completely in Him. He wants us to enter His rest, totally abandoning ourselves to His care. When we are able to believe and say, "God, I trust You," anxiety melts away (p. 20).

How does thinking we are in control (rather than trusting God) create stress?

_____

_____

_____

Read the following Bible verses. How can they reverse stress?

Psalm 37:3

_____

Proverbs 3:5–6

_____

_____

1 Peter 5:6–7

_____

_____

Read the story I tell under "Road Trip!" on pages 20–21. Who are you most like when journeying through life: the husband and wife or the children? Explain.

_____

_____

Rather than stress and worry about the direction we think we're headed in . . . rather than get upset when the road seems difficult . . . rather than wonder why it's taking so long—we can trust our heavenly Father. We can let go of the steering wheel and turn it over to God, trusting that He has a great plan for our lives. I understand that God is the one who sets the course for my life. It took me a long time to fully reach this place of peace, but thankfully, I've finally submitted my entire life to Him (p. 22).

Write a journal entry to illustrate how peaceful and adventurous life can be as passengers who trust our God to guide us on this journey, much like the children on the road trip.

_____

_____

_____

The quickest way to peace is learning to submit every decision in your life to God (p. 22).

Read the passages about Moses (Exodus 32 and 33) I refer to in Chapter 2. Have you made the same decision as Moses: to not go any farther without God? What will you do or not do now that you've made this decision? Use specific examples.

_____

_____

_____

De-Stress Today

Take the "Control Quiz" from pages 26–27.

Each time you answer a or b, write down what you can do to get to answer c. What reminders can you create to help you rely completely on God?

_____

_____

_____

You can start by asking God to show you each time you're trying to take total control, rather than trusting Him. Normally, if I am trying to face a challenge in my own strength, I start to feel tense, and that is an indicator to me that I need to ask for God's help. I suggest you take a few moments each day to pray like this: "Lord, I trust You with the direction of my life, and I give You control today. I'll do my part, and I'll work diligently as You guide me, but I won't receive the stress that comes from thinking I have to have all the answers. I know You have the answers, and I believe You will guide me to do what is right. I trust that You have a great plan for my life."

The next time you're faced with a stressful situation or a difficult decision, don't carry that burden by yourself. Go to God and ask Him to take control. He will reveal to you the right path to take. You may need to be patient, but don't lose faith because God is always faithful.

Go back to the "It's up to me" statements at the beginning of this chapter. Rewrite each statement to show your dependence on God.

_____

_____

_____

_____

_____

_____

_____

_____

Remember...

- Every day we face two options: I trust myself or I trust God.

Some trust in chariots and some in horses, but we trust in the name of the Lord our God. (Psalm 20:7, NIV)

Prayer

God Almighty: I want to learn to lean and depend on You more. I want to totally submit my life to Your will. I want You to guide me in each and every decision I make. Help me to release the need to control everything. I know I'm not in control. Remind me to let You handle this journey. I want to sit in the backseat and enjoy the ride of my life. With You in control, I know everything will work out according to Your plans. I trust You. I love You. I depend solely on You. Amen.

Feel free to add your own personal prayer:

_____

_____

_____

The Best Stress-Relief Possible

Before you begin, please read Chapter 3 in *Overload*.

Get Started

Write about a time this week when you chose to rely on God rather than on yourself. How did it feel? How can you repeat this action throughout the next week?

How do you think confidence can help you remain calm and de-stressed? In whom do you place your confidence? Why?

Review the opening quote from Ralph Waldo Emerson (p. 33). Create a visual to remember the consequences of looking back, around, and up.

Which outlook has been most common for you this week—looking back, around, or up? How has your stress level been as a result of your outlook?

_____

_____

_____

Take the Load Off

The quickest way to beat any problem is to be aware the problem exists, know the answer, and implement the solution *before* it gets out of hand.

Review the examples on pages 33–34. Write why each one helps prevent stress.

Teaching good behavior to younger children versus waiting until they get older.

_____

_____

Maintaining a healthy weight versus going on a crash diet to squeeze into an outfit.

_____

_____

Being alert in class and studying a little each day versus cramming all night for tomorrow's exam.

_____

_____

What is the difference between acting wisely and reacting hurriedly?

_____

_____

Stress, in its most basic form, is a reaction—it's a panic. It is your body's way of saying, "Something bad has happened; I have to fight or flee." In times of real danger, this physical and emotional reaction can be a benefit, but most of the things we stress about aren't real dangers—they're perceived dangers. What if I lose my job? Do they like me? How am I going to get all of this done? These anxieties and hundreds of others trigger your "fight or flight" reflex in an unhealthy, harmful way (p. 34).

Read how the nervous system responds to stress on pages 34–35.

Based on how the body responds to stress, what are some of the potential long-term effects of unmanaged stress on your health?

_____

_____

Every time we become excited, stimulated, or upset, even though we may not realize it, our entire system is gearing up for either fight or flight to defend itself from the perceived threatening or dangerous situation.

I mention above that most of the things we stress about aren't real dangers—they're perceived dangers.

Why do you think we stress about perceived dangers?

_____

_____

Read the section about playing basketball with the best NBA player (p. 36). Imagine yourself in that story. Name the person you think is the greatest basketball player (or the top player in another sport). Now, imagine you are playing the chosen sport with the best player on your team. How confident would you be that you and your teammate could beat another two-person team in a neighborhood game? Explain why you feel this way.

_____

_____

Now, ask yourself a serious question: Do you really believe God is the best player in the game? Do you believe God is in control of your life and helping you play? Explain why and how this could affect your level of stress.

_____

_____

Reflect on the following Scriptures. Jot down themes and thoughts that come to mind.

Jeremiah 29:11–14

_____

_____

2 Chronicles 20:1–30

_____

_____

How do you think praise and worship helped Jehoshaphat and his army face their enemies? Who did they place their confidence in?

_____

_____

De-Stress Today

The promises of God (found throughout the Word of God) are key to stopping stress before it ever begins. When a problem arises, before hitting the panic button and initiating the physical and emotional roller coaster of stress, remember that God has promised that He is going before you and He is going to make a way for you (even when there seems to be no way). Confidence that God is always working in your life is preventive medicine. If you have this confidence, you have implemented a solution before you even get the problem of stress.

What promises from Scripture can you rely on to build your confidence in God's power and ability?

To which situations will you choose to *act* in confidence in God rather than react in panic? Perhaps you are faced with challenges like those listed in *Overload* (a health crisis, a decision to return to work or school, etc.). Try to be mindful that worrying is completely useless and never provides any good benefits. But when you place your faith in God, it opens the door for Him to work!

Remember...

- If God leads you to do something, jump with confidence and live a life that defeats stress before it even starts.

For you have been my hope, Sovereign Lord, my confidence since my youth. From birth I have relied on you; you brought me forth from my mother's womb. I will ever praise you. (Psalm 71:5–6, NIV)

Prayer

Holy God, I thank You for being my hope and my confidence. I know that with You on my team, I have the best player on my side. I have confidence that I can make it. I have confidence that I can defeat stress and live victoriously. When I begin to doubt and take my focus off of You, remind me to trust Your plans and to place my hope in You—and You alone. Amen.

Feel free to add your own words:

I'd Like to Exchange This

Before you begin, please read Chapter 4 in *Overload*.

Get Started

Since reading Chapter 3 and completing the study questions, have you been able to act wisely with confidence in God as opposed to reacting in a panic? Explain how this has or has not impacted your level of stress and well-being. Keep trusting in God and relying on His promises from the Word to build your confidence.

_____

_____

_____

Read the statement that precedes Chapter 4: "Keep Calm and Make a Change." Do you think you need to make any changes to decrease your level of stress? If so, what changes are you contemplating?

_____

_____

_____

Evaluate your life based on the opening quote by Charles Spurgeon (p. 47). How much happiness are you currently enjoying? Rate your happiness level from one to ten (one is the least amount of happiness and ten is the greatest amount). Spend a few moments writing about your rating. What is causing your happiness or lack of it?

_____

_____

_____

Ask yourself: Am I really ready to make a change to decrease my stress and seek more happiness?

Take the Load Off

I love the story about Linda (pp. 47–48). Think about what happens when this busy mom arrives at home, happy to show her sons and husband her new blouse and then realizes it has a rip in the back. Why do you think she didn't want to go through the hassle of returning the blouse?

_____

_____

_____

When have you acted like Linda, refusing to go through the challenge of making an exchange so you could get what you really wanted? Why did you sacrifice your happiness?

_____

_____

_____

Continue to follow the story about Linda when she went out with her girlfriends (pp. 48–49). How did her decision to refuse to exchange the blouse impact her time with friends?

_____

_____

_____

How has your decision to not exchange your stress for happiness impacted your time with loved ones or others?

_____

_____

_____

Stress is kind of like Linda's ripped blouse. It is something that happens often in our lives, through no fault of our own. Linda didn't cause the rip; it just happened. We don't always cause stressful situations; they just happen. Whether you're fifteen, fifty-five, or eighty-five, you're going to deal with stress on a regular basis. And you know what? It's not easy (p. 49).

But there's good news! We do not have to go through life (or through our day) with a "ripped blouse." We can exchange that stress for something better. The Word of God teaches us that we can cast our cares on God (1 Peter 5:7) and exchange the burdens, frustrations, and sorrows of the world for the joy of the Lord (p. 50).

Write how each Scripture applies specifically to you when it comes to exchanging your stress.

> *Be not grieved and depressed, for the joy of the Lord is your strength and stronghold.* (Nehemiah 8:10)

_____

_____

_____

> *To give them beauty for ashes, the oil of joy for mourning, the garment of praise for the spirit of heaviness.* (Isaiah 61:3, NKJV)

_____

_____

_____

> *Weeping may endure for a night, but joy comes in the morning.* (Psalm 30:5)

_____

_____

_____

It's really not that complicated—God wants to make a trade with you. Of course, the ultimate trade is the exchange of your sins for Christ's righteousness (see 2 Corinthians 5:21), but that is just the first in many wonderful exchanges. God wants you to give Him all your cares, problems, and failures. In return, He'll give you His peace and joy. And on top of that, God promises that He is the one who is going to protect and take care of you.

How can you release the stress that robs your peace? What specific steps can you take to stop getting upset about little things that you can't control?

_____

_____

_____

De-Stress Today

Let's revisit Linda's story. How would you rewrite the story about her blouse? Would you exchange it?

_____

_____

_____

Now you have the chance to rewrite your own, true story. How will you make an exchange for the stress you are enduring? Will you decide to give up worrying? Will you put your confidence in God? Will you make a change? (See the lists of practical changes on page 53.)

Are you worshipping or worrying? How can praise and worship refocus your mind and give you peace about your situation? (See page 55 for practical examples on exchanging worry for praise.)

_____

_____

_____

Are you overcommitting yourself? Are you willing to exchange your long list of to-dos for peace? (Read the practical solutions on page 57.)

_____

_____

_____

Whose pace are you moving at? Are you keeping the pace God has set for you or someone else's? Don't waste the energy God has given you trying to do too many things. Use your energy to enjoy the important things God has placed in your life and learn to let some of the other things go.

Remember...

- If you're filled with worry, worship is the key. You can't be a worshipper and a worrier at the same time.

    Peace I leave with you; my peace I give you. I do not give to you as the world gives. Do not let your hearts be troubled and do not be afraid. (John 14:27, NIV)

Prayer

God, I need to make a change. I want to exchange my burdens, worry, and stress for Your peace, love, and joy. Help me to cast all of my cares on You. I'm so grateful that You care and want me to come to You. When I am tempted to carry this burden alone, remind me that You care enough to carry it for me. Give me the tools and wisdom to de-stress and refocus on You. Amen.

Feel free to add your own words:

_____

_____

_____

_____

Leabharlann
6077490
Contae na Midhe

Decisions You Make and Steps You Take

Before you begin, please read Chapter 5 in *Overload*.

Get Started

Reflect on the concept of making an exchange for your stress that we covered in Chapter 4. How have you exchanged stress this past week? What do you need to work on?

_____

_____

_____

Now think about the quote that precedes Chapter 5. In what ways can you try to keep calm and de-stress? Name one particular area you will commit to work on this week.

_____

_____

Find one activity from the "Simple Ways to De-Stress" list on page 62 and try it today. What will you do? What about the rest of the week? Circle the activity for today and those for the rest of the week, and then write in the details (when, with whom, where, etc.). Later, return to this section and note how the activity affected you.

Go for a walk.

_____

_____

Put my phone away.

_____

_____

Watch a funny movie.

_____

_____

Cut back on caffeine.

_____

_____

Write down your worries...then throw them away.

_____

_____

Spend time with a close friend.

_____

_____

Enjoy a new hobby.

_____

_____

Get some exercise.

_____

_____

Plan ahead for tomorrow so you're not so rushed.

_____

_____

Perform a random act of kindness.

_____

_____

Read a good book.

_____

_____

Add additional activities:

_____

_____

Reflect on Lyndon B. Johnson's quote used to open Chapter 5: "Peace is a journey of a thousand miles and it must be taken one step at a time." Contemplate the following: Do you think peace is worth the journey? Explain. How will you remind yourself to take one step at a time on your journey?

_____

_____

In Chapter 5, you will read that "every step you take is important, but perhaps the most important step is the first one."

Why is the first step the most important? Have you taken the first step?

_____

_____

Take the Load Off

The truth is, we don't get to make all the decisions in life. Some things are beyond our control—things like the weather; the amount of traffic;

headlines in the news; or the mood of our spouse, coworkers, children, or friends. We don't get to make any of those external decisions, but that doesn't mean we're victims of our circumstances. We may not be able to choose what happens in the environment around us, but we can certainly choose how we respond to it. And the decisions we make on a daily basis go a long way toward determining the kind of life we are going to live. You can make decisions and you can take steps to change how you view your circumstances and how you respond to them.

Review the suggestions for handling external circumstances on page 64. How would each one make you less stressed if you chose to respond in a similar way?

_____

_____

_____

_____

In what other positive ways could you handle each situation?

_____

_____

_____

Memorize Ralph Waldo Emerson's quote to help you gain control of your perspective on external circumstances: "Nothing external to you has any power over you" (p. 65).

Burdened, overloaded, stressed-out people are focused on the circumstances around them rather than the steps in front of them. Which one are you focused on? Explain.

_____

_____

I want to encourage you today. If you feel burdened or troubled in life, with God's help, you can take a step to change your outlook and overcome your situation. You are not a victim. No matter what you've been through, you don't have to give in to the pain of the past or the pressures of the present. You can decide to take steps in order to live a new life in Christ that is filled with peace and joy (p. 65).

Review and rewrite the Scriptures below in your own words to help you take steps toward de-stressing and finding your peace:

Matthew 19:26

_____

Philippians 4:6–7

_____

Philippians 4:13

_____

Zechariah 4:6

_____

Remember, trusting God and waiting on Him is not a passive activity. There are always steps you can take . . . even when you're waiting on God. Specifically, there are always steps you can take to overcome stress. If you do what you can do, then God will do what you cannot. Do your part to reject every worry and anxiety and God will come through in ways that will amaze you.

Think about a time God came through for you in a way that surpassed your expectations. How did worrying help in that situation? How did doing your part (taking steps) and waiting on God help?

_____

_____

_____

So many people don't take any steps because they don't know *all* the steps, but you don't have to have it all figured out to take an action step. You don't need to worry about the part you don't know how to do—just do the part you know (p. 66).

Think about your current situation and what may be causing stress in your life. What steps can you take to resolve it?

_____

_____

Do your part—and wait and hope and trust in God. You don't have to be prepared to do the entire job by yourself; just prepare yourself to do the best that you can do and remember that God will add what you don't have.

Reread the story of the boy and his lunch in John 6:9–13. How does this story inspire you to do your part and to wait on God for the rest?

_____

_____

For more inspiration, reread the other stories mentioned in Chapter 5. Read them with fresh eyes to see how the stories remind us to be active while waiting on God. Ask God to show you ways you can take action while trusting Him, and write your thoughts below.

Joshua 6:1–20

_____

_____

Luke 8: 40–48

_____

_____

Mark 2:1–5

_____

_____

De-Stress Today

For more useful inspiration, revisit the familiar story of Peter's first steps toward Jesus on the Sea of Galilee in Matthew 14:22–30. Think about how the disciples and Peter felt in the boat with the raging waves. Think about Peter's first step toward Jesus. Even though Peter's faith faltered, it was still greater than any of the other disciples who never got out of the boat. Do you think you are more like Peter or more like the other disciples who stayed in the boat? Explain.

_____

_____

_____

If we take the steps Jesus asks us to take, He will always help us reach our destination.

As long as you focus on the storm rather than on God's promises for life, you're always going to be frustrated, afraid, and stressed out. But God has a better life in store for you. And if you want to live His abundant, confident, joy-filled life, it's time to understand that you have a part to play. You can't sit back in fear and passivity; instead, you can act in faith and take that bold first step (p. 69).

What step will you take today to reclaim or, for the first time, find the abundant, confident, joy-filled life God promises? (For examples, review "Your First Steps to Defeating Stress" on pages 70–72.)

_____

_____

Remember...

- Even though you can't control every situation you face, you can control how you face it.
- You don't have to live a life burdened with stress and frustration. Instead, you can live a happy, peaceful life. It's just a matter of what steps you are going to take. The choice is yours...you get to decide.

With man this is impossible, but with God all things are possible. (Matthew 19:26, NIV)

Prayer

Dear God: I am ready to do my part. Show me how to take practical steps toward de-stressing my life. I know I don't need to know all of the steps. I just need to take one step. I trust You will help me make the rest of the steps when needed. I reject the stressful and overloaded life and receive Your promises for peace and joy. Amen.

Use the lines below to write your own prayer:

_____

_____

_____

Did You Forget Something?

Before you begin, please read Chapter 6 in *Overload*.

Get Started

Review the action steps listed in Chapter 5. Which ones did you take? What happened? How has your faith in God been impacted?

_____

_____

_____

This section is entitled "Keep Calm and Remember God's Goodness." Close your eyes and take a few minutes to think of the ways God has been good to you. Consider how He has blessed you and the challenges He has helped you overcome. Jot down some notes and share your testimony with someone today.

_____

_____

_____

Now that you've thought about your testimony, how does remembering God's goodness help you keep calm and de-stress?

_____

_____

_____

Read Zig Ziglar's quote at the opening of Chapter 6: "It's not the situation, but whether we react negative or respond positive to the situation that is important" (p. 77).

Have you been responding positively or reacting negatively to your situation? Explain.

_____

_____

What can you do to change your course (if you have been reacting negatively) or to stay the course (if you are responding positively)?

_____

_____

Take the Load Off

On pages 77–78, read about how certain noises can stress me out. How did shifting my focus make an annoying sound like a beeping truck turn into a sweet lesson from birds?

_____

_____

_____

What really gets on your nerves? What can you not handle well?

_____

_____

_____

Are there any other things you can focus on when your "noise" occurs? The next time your annoying stressor pops up, how can you shift your focus?

_____

_____

_____

What you focus on will often determine your stress level. One of the biggest causes of stress is focusing on the negative things that are happening around us and allowing those things to fill our hearts with frustration, fear, or anxiety.

Have you ever responded to certain situations like the way I describe in this chapter? Check off the responses you can relate to (p. 79):

_____ If the sink backs up, your day is ruined.

_____ If the car starts to idle funny, you go into a panic.

_____ If your child gets a poor grade in school, you question every parenting decision you've ever made.

Many people get so consumed with what is going wrong that they can't see anything else—their full attention is given solely to their problems. They are convinced that their problems are more difficult than anyone else's. They are consumed with their problems and make dwelling upon them the priority in their lives.

It's really pretty simple: If focusing on what is going wrong is a cause of stress, naturally a cure for stress is to focus on what is right. When we look at the positive things that God has placed in our lives, it gives us a sense of perspective, stability, thankfulness, and balance. And all four of those things are remedies for stress. It is wise and healthy to hold on to the good things in your life and let the negative, stressful things fall by the wayside (p. 80).

Choose five things that are going right in your life and list them below. Try to focus on these things and expand on your list throughout the day.

_____

_____

_____

_____

_____

Read the following verses and describe how they can help us keep our focus on God and God's goodness.

Hebrews 12:2

_____

_____

Colossians 3:2

_____

_____

Philippians 4:8

_____

_____

De-Stress Today

In Philippians 4, Paul doesn't say we should just occasionally think about the good things—he says we are to "fix our minds on them." That means that each and every day, we should take the opportunity to think about what we are thinking about. Rather than dwell on all that is going wrong, we can choose to dwell on all that is going right!

Fill in specific things to focus on as described in Philippians 4:8. Whatever is:

True: _____

Worthy of reverence: _____

Honorable and seemly (appropriate): _____

Just: _____

Pure: _____

Lovely and lovable: _____

Kind: _____

Winsome (sweet): _____

Gracious: _____

Virtuous and excellent: _____

Worthy of praise: _____

Consider creating a graphic with the words listed above to display where you'll see it often. This will help you remember to fix your mind on these positive things to impact your outlook.

What you think about—what you focus on—is going to affect how you see life. If you'll determine to focus on God's goodness and His promises that are "true, pure, lovely, kind, gracious," you won't succumb to the bullying behavior and tactics of stress. When others are frustrated, discouraged, and fed up with their lives, you'll have a totally different attitude. No matter what happens during the course of your day, you'll be able to trust God and respond differently than you used to. You won't be panicked; you'll be peaceful! You won't be overloaded; you'll be overjoyed. That's what happens when you choose to focus on the good things God *has* done and *is* doing on your behalf. You will also be able to encourage those who are focused on negatives. When God gives us His grace to enjoy our lives in the midst of difficulty, it is important to let Him use us to pray for and help those who are still in bondage (p. 81).

Read the list of benefits from Psalm 103 (pp. 84–85). Which benefits do you most need to remember today?

_____

_____

Remember…

- The next time you feel your peace slipping away and your stress picking up steam, take a moment to stop and remember the benefits you've been given as a child of God.

Praise the Lord, my soul; all my inmost being, praise his holy name. Praise the Lord, my soul, and forget not all his benefits. (Psalm 103:1–2, NIV)

Prayer

God, I just want to spend some time thanking You for Your goodness. You have been so very good to me, and I don't want to take anything for granted. I praise You for all You've done. I am humbled by Your amazing love and generosity. Thank You for the gift of eternal and abundant life You've given me through Jesus. Thank You for taking care of me through-out my life. Thank You for providing, even when I didn't know how things would work out. Thank You, thank You, thank You!

Feel free to add your own words of appreciation for the specific things you are grateful for:

_____

_____

_____

Choice Overload

Before you begin, please read Chapter 7 in *Overload*.

Get Started

How has recalling the benefits you've been given as a child of God decreased your stress level? Which benefits have been particularly helpful to remember this week?

_____

_____

_____

Looking back at the past week, are there some things or areas in your life you could have simplified? Explain. How might you simplify similar aspects of the week ahead?

_____

_____

_____

Think about the French proverb at the beginning of Chapter 7: "*Trop de choix tue le choix*" (Too much choice kills the choice). How can too many choices create stress in your life?

_____

_____

_____

*   *   *

Read the three examples of how too much of a good thing can be harmful (pp. 91–92). How have Craig, Jenny, and Sherri used "good things" to their detriment?

_____

_____

_____

Do you have any examples in your life where you've turned a good thing into a bad thing? Share. (I list a few more examples on p. 92.)

_____

_____

_____

Let your moderation be known unto all men. (Philippians 4:5, KJV)

Take the Load Off

The same principle that is true for sleep, food, work, money, ambition, and so on, that all good things in moderation, is also true for the "choices" you and I have in life. I think we both agree that having choices is a good thing, but I've noticed that having too many choices can bring confusion, uncertainty, and a tremendous amount of unnecessary stress. If we allow ourselves to get distracted by the dizzying array of modern options, we can easily fall into the stress trap (pp. 92–93).

But, again, there is good news! If you've ever felt stressed out and overloaded in the face of multiple options, you can be a person who makes wise, bold, confident decisions. You don't have to go through life indecisive and unsure. With God's help, you can cut through the distractions and make strong decisions that will build your peace, not your stress.

Review the five steps to staying calm and making great choices listed on pages 94–101. Then think of a practical way you will incorporate each step into your decision-making process and write about it.

1. **Ask God for Direction:** Any time there is a decision to be made, we can go to God and ask for His guidance and direction.

    _____

    _____

    _____

    So we take comfort and are encouraged and confidently and boldly say, The Lord is my Helper; I will not be seized with alarm [I will not fear or dread or be terrified]. (Hebrews 13:6, AMPC)

2. **Simplify the Decision-Making Process:** We contribute to a lot of the stress we face by making things very complicated and complex. We can be content, slow down, and reduce options to simplify the process.

    _____

    _____

    _____

    Simplicity is so important to enjoying life.

3. **Seek Good Advice:** It's wonderful to be strong and not live your life dependent on what others say, but there are times when the opinions of others can be very beneficial.

    _____

    _____

    _____

    Many times there are people around you who have already gone through what you're facing, and their opinions can be invaluable (p. 98).

4. **Be Confident and Decisive:** Rather than thinking, *What if I get this decision wrong?* choose to have confidence that you will get it right.

_____

_____

_____

Confidence will carry you forward—past doubt, around indecision, and over uncertainty (p. 99).

5. **Let Peace Make the Call:** That feeling of peace is often a confirmation that God is pointing you in that direction. Let peace settle "with finality all questions that arise in your minds" (Colossians 3:15, AMPC).

_____

_____

_____

Which of your options do you have the most peace about? After you've prayed about it, sought wise counsel, discarded the bad options, and confidently considered the best remaining options, what gives you the most peace (p. 100)?

Read the following Scriptures and match them to the ways they can help you when making decisions.

Scriptures	Statements
Proverbs 11:14	I know God's Holy Spirit will guide me into truth.
John 16:13	When I feel peace, I will act.
Colossians 3:15	I can boldly ask God for wisdom and receive it to make decisions.
Philippians 4:11	I will be content with where I am in life, which will make decision-making easier and less stressful.
James 1:5	I will seek out wise advisers when I need help.

De-Stress Today

Think about the analogy of traveling down the Amazon River alone versus with an experienced guide (pp. 101–102). Describe how you would feel traveling alone, and how you would feel with an experienced and trusted guide.

_____

_____

_____

Now remind yourself that you do have an experienced and trusted guide to travel with in life. Write a prayer thanking God for being your guide and asking for help to rely on His direction to make choices.

_____

_____

_____

Ask God to help you see past the distraction of choice overload and trust His guidance. Get ready because He wants to take you on the trip of a lifetime!

Remember...

- When faced with a decision, going to God is a first option, not a last resort.

  I lift up my eyes to the mountains—where does my help come from? My help comes from the Lord, the Maker of heaven and earth. (Psalm 121:-1–2, NIV)

Prayer

Prince of Peace: Teach me how to seek You for decisions I need to make. Help me recognize Your answer and give me peace with each decision. Help me to simplify my life so I can simplify my choices. I am ready for *the trip of my lifetime, so release me from the distractions of choice over-load. I am ready to live a life unencumbered by stress. Amen.*

Feel free to add your own words:

_____

_____

_____

Laugh, Laugh, and Laugh Some More

Before you begin, read Chapter 8 in *Overload*.

Get Started

Did you use the information from Chapter 7 to make any decisions recently? Reflect on the steps you took to make the decision or decisions and the difference in your stress level.

_____

_____

_____

What will you continue to do to reduce stress when making decisions?

_____

_____

_____

Now think about the last time you had a hearty laugh. How did you feel?

_____

_____

_____

Look at the quote by William Thackeray that opens Chapter 8: "A good laugh is sunshine in the house." How does laughter create internal sunshine?

_____

_____

_____

Take the Load Off

When was your last vacation (either at home or away)?

_____

Describe how you felt when you were on vacation.

_____

If you haven't taken a vacation in six months or less, ask yourself why and write down your reasons.

_____

_____

Laughter is like an ignored vacation day—an unused benefit! Unfortunately, laughter is an opportunity that many people neglect to take full advantage of. It's available to all of us—we could enjoy it if we chose to—but it remains in a queue of benefits that is often overlooked. Rather than seeking out opportunities to laugh and enjoying even the smallest things in life, many people go through each day frowning and frustrated—discouragement crowds out delight; problems overshadow playfulness. God has given us the ability to laugh for a reason. It may seem like a little thing, but laughter is vitally important in the battle against stress, anxiety, fear, and worry. It's a tool from God that benefits you in so many ways (p. 108).

Which camp do you find yourself in? Circle where you live most often:

Laughing and enjoying small
things in life

Frowning and frustrated at
problems

How can you move to the laughing and enjoying life camp (or how can you enjoy life even more if you are already there)?

_____

_____

_____

It doesn't matter if it's a night of raucous laughter with hilarious friends, the enjoyment of a funny movie with your family, or even just a giggle over a silly joke—all laughter is a form of stress-relief. It is a physical activity that has nearly unparalleled short-term and long-term benefits for your entire body (p. 109).

Fill in the missing words from Scriptures that encourage laughter.

> He will yet fill your mouth with _____, and your lips with _____. (Job 8:21, NKJV)

> A _____ heart is good _____ and a cheerful _____ works _____, but a broken spirit _____ up the _____. (Proverbs 17:22, AMPC)

> The cheerful _____ has a continual _____. (Proverbs 15:15b, NIV)

> Our mouths were filled with _____, our tongues with songs of _____. Then it was said among the nations, "The _____ has done _____ things for them." (Psalm 126:2, NIV)

Choose a verse from above to memorize so that you can remember the importance of laughter.

De-Stress Today

To intentionally laugh more, choose one of the suggestions I discuss on pages 112–116. Write a specific way you will incorporate your choice into your life today.

Plan to laugh…and then do it. Consider scheduling laughter into your day.

Hang around funny and encouraging people. Name funny people you know.

Change your perspective. Start your morning by deciding to think about something happy or joyful.

Rent or download a funny movie. Try watching a funny video clip.

Laugh at yourself. If you're like me, you probably make some pretty amusing mistakes, too.

Ask God to give you your joy back. Ask God for His help, and ask Him to return His joy to your heart.

Remember…

- No matter what you are going through in life, the joy of the Lord can be your strength. You can have a smile on your face no matter how intimidating the incident, how stressful the situation, or how discouraging the dilemma. We don't laugh over our problems, but we can laugh as we trust God to help us take care of them. The joy of the Lord can ease any emotional and physical ailment and provide you with a new level of satisfaction in life.

Prayer

Dear God: Thank You for the gift of laughter. I desire to use this gift more to reduce my stress and to simply enjoy the life You have given me.

Return joy to me and help me to be satisfied with my life. Help me to laugh at myself and find joy in everyday circumstances. I want to laugh more and to enjoy this day. Amen.

Feel free to add your own words:

_____

_____

_____

The Stress of Comparison

Before you begin, read Chapter 9 in *Overload*.

Get Started

How have you added more laughter to your life after completing Chapter 8?

_____

_____

_____

Share a funny video clip or the name of a funny movie with a person who needs a little more laughter.

Think about the statement that precedes Chapter 9: "Keep Calm and Be Secure." Write about how insecurity can cause stress and how feeling secure brings peace.

_____

_____

_____

Review the list of ways to de-stress that precede Chapter 9 (p. 122).

Place a check mark next to three de-stressing activities you will incorporate into your life today:

_____ Take a deep breath

_____ Listen to praise and worship music

_____ Go to bed on time (maybe even a little early)

_____ Reduce your debt

_____ Forgive someone who hurt you

_____ Take frequent breaks from work

_____ Be playful and laugh a lot

_____ Learn to say no to time demands that will stress you out

_____ Eat more fruit and vegetables

_____ Plan a fun night out

_____ Make a list of things you're thankful for

Think about the quote by Charles Spurgeon (p. 123). Evaluate your life. On a scale of one to ten, how much are you enjoying your life (one is not much; ten is to the fullest)? Draw a scale with numbers one through ten and place your needle on the number you selected.

Now write about ways you can move the needle closer to ten.

_____

_____

_____

Take the Load Off

Reacquaint yourself with the story of David and Goliath by reading 1 Samuel 17:1–50. Consider using a Bible app to read the Scriptures from a modern language translation, such as the Contemporary English Version or the Message.

Think about how the outcome of this story would have been different if David had allowed the comparisons to stop him from pursuing Goliath the way he knew how to fight.

What could have happened if he wore the same armor as Saul or the other soldiers?

_____

_____

What would have happened if David acted like the other soldiers and thought Goliath was too big to fight?

_____

_____

No matter how hard others tried to get David to fight like Saul, the most important thing David could do was to be himself.

How did David gain security to fight Goliath?

_____

_____

_____

How can you gain security to stop comparing yourself or your journey to others?

_____

_____

_____

The more you compare your life to those around you, the less you'll enjoy the life God has given you. Nothing good comes from trying to imitate, compete with, or outdo someone else.

Write a prayer, asking God to show you times you've sacrificed peace and security by comparing yourself to others. Confess them and ask for help to live your best life—and to enjoy it.

_____

_____

_____

De-Stress Today

Take a few moments and answer these questions about yourself. Pray for God to help you be honest with yourself.

What do you think of yourself?

_____

_____

_____

How do you feel about who you are?

_____

_____

_____

Do you ever compare yourself with other people and feel discouraged if you can't do what they can do or be like them?

_____

_____

_____

Have you ever said, "I wish I looked like her," or "I wish I had what they have," or "I wish I could do what you do"? Theodore Roosevelt said, "Comparison is the thief of joy." The more you are comfortable with *you*, the more joy you will have.

We don't have to live insecure lives, because it's God's will for us to be very secure and not to live in fear. We were created to feel safe, secure, confident, and bold; it's part of our spiritual DNA as born-again believers in Christ. But the key to living a secure life in Christ is knowing who you are in Christ, really receiving God's love for you, and basing your worth and value on who God says you are (p. 128).

Now think about what God says about you in His Word. Read each of the following Scriptures and rewrite them in your own words:

Psalm 139: 13–14

_____

_____

_____

John 3:16

_____

_____

_____

1 John 4:12–19

_____

_____

_____

Romans 8:38–39

_____

_____

_____

Rather than finding your identity by comparing yourself with another, ask God to help you confidently find your identity in Him.

On pages 130–131, review the ways to remember your identity in God each and every day.

Remember…

- We were created to feel safe, secure, confident, and bold: these are parts of our spiritual DNA as born-again believers in Christ (p. 128).

  For I am convinced that neither death nor life, neither angels nor demons, neither the present nor the future, nor any powers, neither height nor depth, nor anything else in all creation, will be able to separate us from the love of God that is in Christ Jesus our Lord. (Romans 8:38–39, NIV)

Prayer

My Lord and My God: Forgive me for comparing myself to others. Forgive me for wishing I were different. Help me to embrace who You've created me to be. Help me to see the gifts and talents and uniqueness You've given to me. Help me to know who I am in You and to walk confidently throughout life. I want to have joy and I want to feel secure and safe in You. Amen.

Feel free to add your own words:

_____

_____

_____

_____

Change the Conversation

Before you begin, please read Chapter 10 in *Overload*.

Get Started

Reflect on whether or not you've made progress in breaking the stressful pattern of comparing yourself to others. What helped? What do you still need to work on to feel loved and secure in who God created you to be?

_____

_____

_____

_____

How can watching what you say help alleviate stress?

_____

_____

Think about the last compliment you received. How did it make you feel?

_____

_____

_____

What do you think George Herbert meant when he said, "Good words are worth much, and cost little" (p. 137)?

_____

_____

_____

   Words can lift us into ecstasy or they can cause some of the worst emotional pain we can feel as humans (p. 137).

Take the Load Off

The words you speak each day are an indication of the kind of life you are going to live. If your conversations are positive, hope-filled, and full of encouragement, you are going to face that day with a certain level of joy and optimism. However, if your conversations are despair-riddled, stress-filled, and burdened by doubt, you are probably in for a long day...a very long, stressful day.

   Think about your conversations. Are they more likely to be positive and hope-filled or negative and stress-filled? Circle one.

Positive and hope-filled   Negative and stress-filled

   Why do you think your conversations trend the way they do? What changes can you make?

_____

_____

   Keep a log of your conversations for one day. What positive words did you speak? What negative words did you voice?

Positive words	Negative words

Words are wonderful when used in the proper way. They can encourage, edify, and give confidence to the hearer. A right word spoken at the right time can actually be life-changing. We can literally increase our own joy and greatly reduce stress by speaking right words. We can also upset ourselves by talking unnecessarily about our problems or about things that have hurt us in relationships. I wonder how many people who are seriously stressed out ever consider that a large part of it may be caused by their own conversation (p. 139)?

Read the following Scriptures and rewrite them in your own words to help you remember to watch your words and increase your joy rather than your stress level:

Proverbs 16:24

_____

_____

Psalm 19:14

_____

_____

Proverbs 15:23

_____

_____

Reflect on this statement on page 145: It is quite possible to avoid a lot of our stress by just making an effort to not talk unless we truly have something worthy of being said.

How could you reduce your stress level by following this advice?

_____

_____

_____

De-Stress Today

To reduce stress in your life, take the time to be mindful of God's promises and scriptural encouragements. Read the following Scriptures and fill in the missing words. Memorize your favorite Scriptures to help you be more mindful of God's promises.

Give _____ to him and _____ his name. For the Lord is _____ and his love endures _____; his _____ continues through all generations. (Psalm 100:4–5, NIV)

And let us consider how we may spur one another on toward _____ and good _____, not giving up meeting together, as some are in the habit of doing, but _____ one another—and all the more as you see the Day approaching. (Hebrews 10:24–25, NIV)

Lord, who may dwell in your sacred tent?...The one whose walk is _____, who does what is _____, who speaks the _____ from their heart. (Psalm 15:1–2, NIV)

Maybe you've never really thought about the words you were speaking each day. Or maybe you've fallen into the habit of rehearsing your problems and speaking negative, discouraging words and didn't even know you were doing it. Whatever the case, I want to encourage you to make a fresh start today. It's never too late to change your conversation. Use the effective tool God has given you to battle stress: your words (p. 146).

Remember…

- Talking too much can disturb our peace and cause stress.
- Rather than rehearse your problems, it's time to start reciting God's goodness.

Practice reciting God's goodness below. List five things you have to be grateful for today.

_____

_____

_____

_____

Recite your list whenever you are tempted to rehearse your problems.

Prayer

God: I desire to speak words that bring life. I desire to use my words to praise You and to speak of Your goodness. Help me to watch what I say. Help me to stop using careless and reckless words. I don't want to rehearse my problems; instead I want to use my words to defeat stress and uplift You, myself, and others. Amen.

Feel free to add your own positive words:

_____

_____

It Is Well with My Soul

Before you begin, read Chapter 11 in *Overload*.

Get Started

Evaluate how you've changed your conversation since reading Chapter 10. Has your stress level changed? Explain.

_____

_____

Think about your life for a few minutes. Do you enjoy your journey, or are you preoccupied, stressed, or worried about life issues? Explain.

_____

_____

_____

Consider whether you agree with the quote by Will Rogers at the beginning of this chapter: "Half of our life is spent trying to find something to do with the time we have rushed through life trying to save." Explain why or why not.

_____

_____

_____

On pages 151–152, read the example of the difference between Dave's attitude and my attitude in the early years of my ministry. Does your attitude tend to be more like Dave's (joyful, content, and carefree) or more like mine (frustrated, upset, or stressed)? Explain.

_____

_____

_____

We can decide whether we want to be stressed out or not. We can choose to be joyful . . . we can choose to be content . . . and we can choose to love life regardless of the circumstances around us (p. 152).

Write a letter to yourself describing how you choose to feel today and why:

_____

_____

_____

_____

Take the Load Off

Enjoying life begins with enjoying yourself. Think about whether or not you enjoy yourself. What can you do to begin to enjoy yourself more?

_____

_____

_____

We can make our days stressful by trying to control what everyone does (p. 155).

Is this true of you? Explain. If so, how can you learn to focus on controlling yourself rather than other people?

_____

_____

_____

Giving others freedom brings peace into our relationships and helps us enjoy our journey through life.

No one is perfect. We are all a work in progress. Keep moving forward one step at a time. You don't have to be stressed by how far you still have to go—all you need to do is keep going. In a few sentences, describe your own journey and your ultimate goals, including how far you've come and what you plan to do to keep moving forward.

_____

_____

_____

_____

Remember that you can be extraordinarily happy while living an ordinary, everyday life (p. 157). Expecting life to be one long series of exciting events is setting yourself up for disappointment. How do you think expecting lots of excitement can lead to stress and disappointment?

_____

_____

_____

Start your days by saying, "Good morning, Lord!" "This is the day the Lord has made. I will rejoice and be glad in it" (Psalm 118:24).

Write out and decorate the words from Psalm 118 to remind you to welcome God into each day. Keep the graphic on your computer, phone, desk, or another place where you will view it often. Rejoice each time you see the verse.

Find a video of "It Is Well with My Soul" online or sing the song aloud. Think about the story of Horatio Spafford (pp. 158–159). How can his story inspire you to keep going in the midst of trouble and seek to enjoy life amid your pain?

_____

_____

_____

A struggle or a personal loss doesn't have to overshadow every part of your life. You can still have joy even in the midst of sorrow (pp. 159–160).

De-Stress Today

Write *God, I trust You* over and over again until you believe it. Repeat this exercise whenever you need to boost your faith and decrease your stress.

_____

_____

_____

_____

Look up the wording for Romans 8:28 in at least three different translations of the Bible. Memorize your favorite version.

_____

_____

_____

Trust God today.

Remember...

- Keep choosing happiness until it becomes second nature. You'll start to feel better and have less stress.
- Dread is a close relative of fear, and allowing it to remain in your mind sets you up for misery and robs you of joy. In order to enjoy your life, it is essential to give special attention to your attitude.

I will praise the Lord at all times. I will constantly speak his praises.
(Psalm 34:1, NLT)

Prayer

Almighty God: I desire to praise You at all times—when I feel good and hopeful and when I don't. Teach me to turn to You in all situations and to seek Your face. I don't want the circumstances of life to steal my joy and make me miserable. Regardless of what I'm facing, I desire to hope in You and to trust You. Amen.

Feel free to add your own words:

_____

_____

_____

Facing Stress Head-on!

Before you begin, read Chapter 12 in *Overload*.

Get Started

How have you been enjoying your life more since reading Chapter 11? List at least three specific ways.

_____

_____

_____

What changes do you think you still need to make to decrease stress and increase joy in your life?

_____

_____

_____

How can making a plan help you implement these changes? Write some ways you can start planning now.

_____

_____

_____

Take the Load Off

Review the action plan steps suggested on pages 168–177. Respond to each question honestly.

1. **Start Your Day by Spending Time with God**

    How do you begin your day now? What can you do to start (or increase your quality of time) with God each day?

    _____

    _____

    _____

    God doesn't want to just be the button we push when we have an emergency (p. 169).

2. **Exercise**

    How often do you exercise each week? What are some specific ways you can incorporate more exercise (even in five- to ten-minute increments) into your day and week? What exercises do you enjoy—or what exercises would you like to try? Don't discount the benefits of a brisk walk.

    _____

    _____

    _____

    When you experience stress, one of the best things you can do is pretty simple: move! Exercise is a terrific physical solution to stress (p. 170).

3. **Make Sure You're Getting Enough Sleep**

    How much sleep do you get on average each night? How can you increase this amount, if needed?

_____

_____

_____

Develop the practice of regular sleep and you will enjoy your life much more (p. 172).

4. **Take a Vacation**

What keeps you from taking more frequent vacations? How can you change this and plan a vacation soon? You can enjoy time at home or on a trip to relax and refuel.

_____

_____

_____

I've learned to plan for and schedule days when I do nothing that is work related. This is the healthy thing to do, and in the long run, it makes me a better and more productive worker. Vacation is more than a company benefit; it's a life benefit (p. 173).

5. **Give Yourself a Reward**

What treat will you give yourself when you meet a short-term goal related to decreasing the stress in your life?

_____

_____

_____

Just the knowledge that you are successfully reaching your goals may be enough to motivate you, but give yourself a little reward anyway. It's a great stress-reducer (p. 174).

6. **Evaluate Your Influences**

Who or what—people, books, music, events—is influencing your life? Is that influence making your life less stressful or is it making your life more stressful?

_____

_____

_____

Name a few people who can make your life less stressful, or things you enjoy that can do the same. Plan to include them in your life more often.

_____

_____

_____

Quite often the decisions we have to make in order to reduce our stress are not easy ones, but in the long run the benefit outweighs the difficulty (p. 175).

7. **Do Less, Not More**

How many times do you hear yourself say, "I'm busy"? Whose pace are you moving at? Is it a pace God has set for you or someone else's pace?

_____

_____

_____

How can you avoid the stress of following someone else's pace and yield to God's Holy Spirit for direction?

_____

_____

_____

Allow God's Spirit to lead you out of a stressful lifestyle and into one of peace and joy (p. 177).

De-Stress Today

Read each Scripture and write how each one can help you follow one or more of the action steps suggested above.

Matthew 11:28–30

_____

_____

_____

Zechariah 4:6

_____

_____

_____

3 John 2

_____

_____

_____

1 Timothy 4:8

_____

_____

_____

Proverbs 18:24

_____

_____

_____

Ecclesiastes 9:7–10

_____

_____

_____

Remember...

- A vacation is a strategically planned and executed event that will ultimately refresh your mind and your body.
- God wants us to burn *on*, not burn *out*!
- It's important to take action in life. Sitting back and passively wishing stress would go away won't work. Ask God to help you make a plan and then aggressively put that plan into action.

Prayer

Merciful and loving God: I desire to live the joyful life You've promised me. Help me to develop an action plan to release stress and live according to Your plans and Your pace. Show me where I need to change. Give me the wisdom, courage, and strength to put Your plan into action. I am eternally grateful to You. Amen.

Add any additional words you'd like:

_____

_____

_____

Seeing Things Differently

Before you begin, read Chapter 13 in *Overload*.

Get Started

How have you worked on your plan of action to decrease stress? What has worked well? What has not worked well? What adjustments do you need to make?

_____

_____

_____

Review the "Simple Ways to De-Stress" list that precedes Chapter 13. Circle the ones you will do this week.

Make a list of things you're thankful for
Drink more water
Take the afternoon off
Slow down
Block stressful people from your Facebook newsfeed
Reevaluate your calendar
Get organized
Think about something pleasant

Forgive yourself

Smile more

Finish one project before starting another

Do something you enjoy

Now consider a few more simple ways you can de-stress and write them below:

_____

_____

_____

Reflect on the quote at the beginning of Chapter 13 from J. G. Holland: "Calmness is the cradle of power." Journal for a few moments about the meaning of the quote and how it impacts your life.

_____

_____

_____

_____

Take the Load Off

How can a new vantage point produce a new attitude?

_____

_____

Now read the examples of biblical figures who faced stress but didn't give in to it. Reread their stories from the Bible and think of reasons they were able to overcome stress.

How did Daniel face the lions without panicking and screaming in terror? (Read Daniel 6:1–23.)

_____

_____

_____

How did Moses stand before Pharaoh without suffering an anxiety attack? (Read Exodus 5–7.)

_____

_____

How could Ruth remain so calm when her husband died and she had nowhere to go? (Read Ruth 1.)

_____

_____

How could Paul preach the Gospel in the face of tremendous opposition without being overcome with stress? (Read Acts 17:1–15.)

_____

_____

_____

Our perspective, up to this point, has often been that we have to handle this stress on our own—we have to fix the problem; we have to find a way to remove those things that stress us. But this self-reliant perspective only makes things worse. Our bodies were created by God to withstand a certain amount of stress, but when we push ourselves beyond that limit, we begin to experience problems (p. 183).

When we continue stretching ourselves to the limit, like a rubber band, one day we snap.

What tangible reminders, like a rubber band, can you use to remember to change your perspective and not give way to stress?

_____

_____

_____

Place one or more of these reminders on your desk (or another place you will see it often) today.

De-Stress Today

Rewrite John 14:27 in your own words to remind yourself to change your perspective when you are faced with stress.

_____

_____

The right mind-set and the right attitude can completely turn a situation around (p. 185).

Journal about a time when your perspective changed the way you handled a situation that could have been stressful.

_____

_____

_____

_____

How can you remember to take this perspective more often?

_____

_____

_____

How many times have you said no to something you didn't feel peace about doing? How can you say no more often when you do not have peace?

_____

_____

_____

Learn to recognize the symptoms of stress when they first show up in you, and instead of making excuses, ask God to help you deal with it properly. If that means not doing something you would like to do, then follow God's peace and wisdom, and you will benefit by not having the draining effects of stress (p. 188).

*   *   *

Practice peace by memorizing the following verses from the Bible. Fill in the blanks below to get you started on memorizing them:

Be _____ and _____ that I am _____. (Psalm 46:10, NIV)

Oh, that their _____ would be inclined to _____ me and keep all my _____ always so that it might go _____ with them and their _____ forever. (Deuteronomy 5:29, NIV)

Do not be _____ about anything, but in every situation, by _____ and _____, with thanksgiving, present your requests to _____. And the _____ of God, which transcends all _____, will guard your hearts and your _____ in Christ Jesus. (Philippians 4:6–7, NIV)

Remember…

- Regardless of how difficult your boss is, how frustrating the leaky faucet is, how low the bank account sinks…God has a great plan for your life.
- If you'll take time each day to get a proper perspective and trust God's plan for your life, the little things that try to bring stress into your life won't seem so important anymore.

Therefore, since we are surrounded by such a great cloud of witnesses, let us throw off everything that hinders and the sin that so easily entangles. And let us run with perseverance the race marked out for us, fixing our eyes on Jesus, the pioneer and perfecter of faith. For the joy set before him he endured the cross, scorning its shame, and sat down at the right hand of the throne of God. Consider him who endured such opposition from sinners, so that you will not grow weary and lose heart. (Hebrews 12:1–3, NIV)

Prayer

Holy God: I know You've given strength to the "cloud of witnesses" in the past. I know You've done mighty acts and provided strength for challenges. I believe You can give me the same courage and strength to face big and small challenges today without stressing. Remind me to rely on You each step of the way so that I might live a life filled with joy and not one overloaded with stress. I am grateful for all You've done and all You promise to continue doing. Amen.

Feel free to add your own words:

_____

_____

_____

The Quickest Way to Defeat Stress

Before you begin, read Chapter 14 in *Overload*.

Get Started

Have you ever blessed someone and felt blessed in return? Explain.

_____

_____

_____

Explain what you think the quote by John Bunyan means (p. 197): "You have not lived today until you have done something for someone who can never repay you."

_____

_____

_____

Why do you think an obsession with self is a breeding ground for stress, pressure, and anxiety?

_____

_____

_____

Likewise, why do you think people who often have their "faces to the coal" do not need applause from others? (See the story on pages 197–198.)

_____

_____

_____

Take the Load Off

Love always requires action. It's not just a thing we try to get for ourselves, but instead it is an action we express to others through doing something, like sharing and serving. Love is much more than a word, or a theory; it is an action (p. 198).

How are you giving love to others through sharing and serving?

_____

_____

How do you give love to:

God

And you shall love the Lord your God with all your [mind and] heart and with your entire being and with all your might. (Deuteronomy 6:5, AMPC)

_____

_____

We want to spend time with those we love, so it stands to reason that loving God will display itself in wanting to spend time with Him. I like the thought of "doing life with God"—including Him in everything I do and talking with Him throughout each day. Being obedient to God's will is one of the highest forms of showing love for Him (p. 199).

Yourself

You shall love your neighbor as yourself. (Mark 12:31, AMPC)

_____

_____

_____

How can you or I love someone else if we don't even know how to love ourselves? This is why God wants us to accept ourselves, embrace our personalities and even our imperfections, knowing that although we are not where we need to be, we are making progress (p. 200).

Others

He who does not love abides (remains, is held and kept continually) in [spiritual] death. (1 John 3:14, AMPC)

_____

_____

_____

Loving others is the only way to keep the God-kind of life flowing through you. God's love is a gift to us; it's in us, but we need to release it to others through words and actions (p. 201).

Practice what I call "loving out loud." Let love be loud in your life. Do it often and aggressively. Challenge yourself to think of three people who could really use a gesture of God's love. Write down their names and something you can do this week to show God's love to them (see page 205 for suggestions).

_____

_____

_____

_____

_____

_____

After you have showed love to these three people, take some time to record how you felt.

_____

_____

_____

Now, try to love out loud each day and show someone love.

De-Stress Today

Assess your life: Are you more focused on yourself or others? Explain.

_____

_____

_____

Perhaps you need to learn what I had to learn, that you'll never be happy and have peace until you learn to love others and serve them like Jesus.

Reflect on how Jesus loves to the "last and highest degree" (John 13:1). How can we imitate that love?

_____

_____

_____

Fill in the blanks for the love Scripture in 1 Corinthians 13:4–8 (NIV). What areas do you need to work on to show more love?

Love is _____ love is _____. It does not _____, it does not _____, it is not _____. It does not _____ others, it is not

_____, it is not easily _____, it keeps no record of _____. Love does not delight in _____ but rejoices with the _____. It always _____, always _____, always _____, always _____. Love never _____.

What is the difference between a martyr and a servant? Which one are you?

_____

_____

_____

Remember...

- When you serve others, joy is restored, peace reigns, stress is lowered, and God is pleased.
- Look for ways to encourage; look for ways to bless—even though the demands in your life seem pressing.

So in everything, do to others what you would have them do to you.
(Matthew 7:12, NIV)

Prayer

My Lord and My God: Thank You for Your amazing love toward me. Thank You for Your ultimate sacrifice of Christ for me. Thank You for all of the gifts You've bestowed upon me. Help me to learn to love You by serving others. Even when I feel bogged down with life's demands, keep me mindful of Your commandment to love my neighbor. Help me to show Your love through my actions and service for others. I desire to share this amazing love You've given to me. Amen.

Feel free to add your own words.

_____

_____

_____

_____

The First Day of the Rest of Your Life

Before you begin, please read Chapter 15 in *Overload*.

Get Started

How have you put love into action since reading Chapter 14?

_____

_____

_____

How has blessing others impacted your stress levels? Explain.

_____

_____

_____

Consider whether you agree with the opening quote by Joseph Addison: "A contented mind is the greatest blessing a man can enjoy in this world." Write your thoughts below.

_____

_____

_____

Now that you've read all fifteen chapters of *Overload*, what areas of your life do you think you need to work on to reduce stress? Write notes below the subjects you want to focus on.

Defeat stress with specific methods to de-stress.

_____

Remember that God is in control.

_____

Put my confidence in God.

_____

Exchange my cares for God's peace.

_____

Choose how to take a step.

_____

Remember my benefits and blessings.

_____

Reduce my choices.

_____

Laugh more often.

_____

Stop comparing myself to others.

_____

Change my conversation.

_____

Choose to hope no matter the circumstances.

_____

Face stress head-on.

_____

Change my perspective.

_____

Bless others more often.

_____

Take the Load Off

Do you believe that God allows do-overs? Explain.

_____

_____

Are you ready to make a fresh start in life to reduce stress and enjoy each day? How will you make a fresh start?

_____

_____

_____

Revisit pages 215–216, focusing on the text about biblical figures listed. Share how they were given do-overs. You may also add your favorite Bible figure's story.

Moses

_____

_____

David

_____

_____

Gideon

_____

_____

Peter

_____

_____

Paul

_____

_____

Mary of Magdala

_____

_____

Others

_____

_____

Regardless of the pain, the pressure, the anxiety, or the stress you've been living with, God wants to give you a brand-new start (p. 226).

Meditate on 2 Corinthians 5:17. Read it from several Bible translations if you can. What does this verse mean to you? How does it remind you that you can have a do-over and start living life differently?

_____

_____

_____

_____

Choosing to live with joy doesn't mean that we never experience any negative emotions like anger, sadness, or disappointment. It does mean that we have a choice not to let them rule us. Most of the emotions that we experience in life are very normal and even necessary. We can choose to let our emotions rule our behavior or to manage them in such a way that, although we don't deny their existence, we do deny them the right to control us (p. 217).

Which one will you choose today? Circle one.

Let my emotions rule and   or   Deny my emotions the right
   govern my behavior   to control me

Write ways you will incorporate my suggestions to remain stable and enjoy your life.

1. **Choose to Live with Hope**

    Expecting good and living with a positive attitude are great stress relievers (p. 218).

    _____

    _____

    _____

    Be a prisoner of hope.

2. **Press on . . . Even When It's Difficult**

    To reap right results in life, you must decide to do right when you don't feel like it (p. 220).

    _____

    _____

    _____

    It's time for you to take charge of your life and follow God's will instead of bowing down to pressure that is designed to prevent you from living out your destiny (p. 221).

3. **Focus on How Far You've Come Already**

    Look at all God has done in your life rather than seeing all you have yet to do.

    _____

    _____

    _____

    Jesus is not only with you, but He is also for you (p. 224).

4. **Never Give Up**

    Keep on keeping on!

    _____

    _____

    _____

    Whatever you may be facing or experiencing in your life right now, stay positive and refuse to go back to those anxious, worried, stress-filled mind-sets. God is with you (p. 225).

De-Stress Today

Read the list of simple ways to de-stress from page 228. Circle the activities you will incorporate into your life this week.

Take a nap

Enjoy a delicious, nutritious meal

Do something special for yourself

Make a list of your strengths

Volunteer to do something that will help someone else

Count your blessings

Call a friend who has a way of encouraging you

Play with your dog (if you don't have a dog, play with your neighbor's dog)

Get outdoors for a while

Cut back on your caffeine intake

Eat less sugar

Turn off your electronics for an hour

Read uplifting material

Smile for no reason in particular

Write about your new beginning and how you will live a joyful life rather than a stress-filled one.

_____

_____

_____

_____

_____

Do not conform to the pattern of this world, but be transformed by the renewing of your mind. Then you will be able to test and approve what God's will is—his good, pleasing and perfect will. (Romans 12:2, NIV)

Remember...

- Regardless of the pain, the pressure, the anxiety, or the stress you've been living with, God wants to give you a brand-new start.
- If we wait patiently, pressing on even when things get difficult, God will always show up and do what we could not do on our own.

"For I know the plans I have for you," declares the Lord, "plans to prosper you and not to harm you, plans to give you hope and a future." (Jeremiah 29:11, NIV)

Prayer

God, I thank You for a new beginning. I thank You for loving me so much that You want the very best for me. I vow to live the abundant life Jesus died to give me. I will keep pressing on and holding on to Your hand as I refocus and allow You to renew my mind each day. I will not give up or give in to the pressures of life. I desire more and I receive more peace, love, and joy from You. Amen.

Feel free to add your own words:

_____

_____

_____

Do you have a real relationship with Jesus?

God loves you! He created you to be a special, unique, one-of-a-kind individual, and He has a specific purpose and plan for your life. And through a personal relationship with your Creator—God—you can discover a way of life that will truly satisfy your soul.

No matter who you are, what you've done, or where you are in your life right now, God's love and grace are greater than your sin—your mistakes. Jesus willingly gave His life so you can receive forgiveness from God and have new life in Him. He's just waiting for you to invite Him to be your Savior and Lord.

If you are ready to commit your life to Jesus and follow Him, all you have to do is ask Him to forgive your sins and give you a fresh start in the life you are meant to live. Begin by praying this prayer...

Lord Jesus, thank You for giving Your life for me and forgiving me of my sins so I can have a personal relationship with You. I am sincerely sorry for the mistakes I've made, and I know I need You to help me live right.

Your Word says in Romans 10:9, "If you declare with your mouth, 'Jesus is Lord,' and believe in your heart that God raised him from the dead, you will be saved" (NIV). I believe You are the Son of God and confess You as my Savior and Lord. Take me just as I am, and work in my heart, making me the person You want me to be. I want to live for You, Jesus, and I am so grateful that You are giving me a fresh start in my new life with You today.

I love You, Jesus!

It's so amazing to know that God loves us so much! He wants to have a deep, intimate relationship with us that grows every day as we spend time with Him in prayer and Bible study. And we want to encourage you in your new life in Christ.

Please visit joycemeyer.org/salvation to request Joyce's book *A New Way of Living*, which is our gift to you. We also have other free resources online to help you make progress in pursuing everything God has for you.

Congratulations on your fresh start in your life in Christ! We hope to hear from you soon.

JOYCE MEYER is one of the world's leading practical Bible teachers. Her daily broadcast, *Enjoying Everyday Life*, airs on hundreds of television networks and radio stations worldwide.

Joyce has written more than one hundred inspirational books. Her best-sellers include *Power Thoughts*; *The Confident Woman*; *Look Great, Feel Great*; *Starting Your Day Right*; *Ending Your Day Right*; *Approval Addiction*; *How to Hear from God*; *Beauty for Ashes*; and *Battlefield of the Mind*.

Joyce travels extensively, holding conferences throughout the year and speaking to thousands around the world.

Joyce Meyer Ministries
P.O. Box 655
Fenton, MO 63026
USA
(636) 349-0303

Joyce Meyer Ministries—Canada
P.O. Box 7700
Vancouver, BC V6B 4E2
Canada
(800) 868-1002

Joyce Meyer Ministries—Australia
Locked Bag 77
Mansfield Delivery Centre
Queensland 4122
Australia
(07) 3349 1200

Joyce Meyer Ministries—England
P.O. Box 1549
Windsor SL4 1GT
United Kingdom
01753 831102

Joyce Meyer Ministries—South Africa
P.O. Box 5
Cape Town 8000
South Africa
(27) 21-701-1056

OTHER BOOKS BY JOYCE MEYER

100 Ways to Simplify Your Life
21 Ways to Finding Peace and Happiness
Any Minute
Approval Addiction
The Approval Fix
The Battle Belongs to the Lord
Battlefield of the Mind*
Battlefield of the Mind for Kids
Battlefield of the Mind for Teens
Battlefield of the Mind Devotional
Be Anxious for Nothing*
Being the Person God Made You to Be
Beauty for Ashes
Change Your Words, Change Your Life
The Confident Mom
The Confident Woman
The Confident Woman Devotional
Do Yourself a Favor…Forgive
Eat the Cookie…Buy the Shoes
Eight Ways to Keep the Devil Under Your Feet
Ending Your Day Right
Enjoying Where You Are on the Way to Where You Are Going
Filled with the Spirit
Good Health, Good Life
Hearing from God Each Morning
How to Hear from God*
How to Succeed at Being Yourself
I Dare You
If Not for the Grace of God*
In Pursuit of Peace
The Joy of Believing Prayer
Knowing God Intimately
A Leader in the Making
Life in the Word
Living Beyond Your Feelings
Living Courageously
Look Great, Feel Great
Love Out Loud
The Love Revolution
Making Good Habits, Breaking Bad Habits
Making Marriage Work (previously published as *Help Me—I'm Married!*)
Me and My Big Mouth!*
The Mind Connection*
Never Give Up!
Never Lose Heart
New Day, New You

*Overload**
The Penny
Perfect Love (previously published as *God Is Not Mad at You*)*
The Power of Being Positive
The Power of Being Thankful
The Power of Determination
The Power of Forgiveness
The Power of Simple Prayer
Power Thoughts
Power Thoughts Devotional
Reduce Me to Love
The Secret Power of Speaking God's Word
The Secrets of Spiritual Power
The Secret to True Happiness
Seven Things That Steal Your Joy
Start Your New Life Today
Starting Your Day Right
Straight Talk
Teenagers Are People Too!
Trusting God Day by Day
The Word, the Name, the Blood
Woman to Woman
You Can Begin Again

JOYCE MEYER SPANISH TITLES

Belleza en Lugar de Cenizas (Beauty for Ashes)
Buena Salud, Buena Vida (Good Health, Good Life)
Cambia Tus Palabras, Cambia Tu Vida (Change Your Words, Change Your Life)
El Campo de Batalla de la Mente (Battlefield of the Mind)
Como Formar Buenos Habitos y Romper Malos Habitos
(Making Good Habits, Breaking Bad Habits)
La Conexión de la Mente (The Mind Connection)
Dios No Está Enojado Contigo (God Is Not Mad at You)
La Dosis de Aprobación (The Approval Fix)
Empezando Tu Día Bien (Starting Your Day Right)
Hazte Un Favor a Ti Mismo…Perdona (Do Yourself a Favor…Forgive)
Madre Segura de sí Misma (The Confident Mom)
Pensamientos de Poder (Power Thoughts)
Sobrecarga (Overload)
Termina Bien tu Día (Ending Your Day Right)
Usted Puede Comenzar de Nuevo (You Can Begin Again)
Viva Valientemente (Living Courageously)

*Study Guide available for this title

BOOKS BY DAVE MEYER

Life Lines